Transformed

The Journey from Despair to Extreme Hope

Life is prettier in Pink!

LIFE STRATEGIST IMAGINATOR

Through the Eyes of Compassion
Life is prettier in Pink!
© 2020 by Lori Clifton

Cover design by: SpeakTruth Media Group LLC
Cover image credit: Visiva Studio, Italy through Shutterstock

Scripture quotations marked TPT are from The Passion Translation®. Copyright © 2017, 2018 by Passion & Fire Ministries, Inc. Used by permission. All rights reserved. ThePassionTranslation.com.

Scriptures marked AMP are taken from the AMPLIFIED BIBLE (AMP): Scripture taken from the AMPLIFIED® BIBLE, Copyright © 1954, 1958, 1962, 1964, 1965, 1987 by the Lockman Foundation Used by Permission. (www.Lockman.org)

Scriptures marked NIV are taken from the NEW INTERNATIONAL VERSION (NIV): Scripture taken from THE HOLY BIBLE, NEW INTERNATIONAL VERSION ®. Copyright© 1973, 1978, 1984, 2011 by Biblica, Inc.™. Used by permission of Zondervan

Published by:

www.speaktruthmedia.com
PO Box 1448, Crockett TX 75835-7448

For information about special discounts available for bulk purchases, sales promotions, fundraising, and educational needs, contact by email: SpeakTruth Media Group LLC at order@speaktruthmedia.com.

ISBN (pb) 978-1-7342646-9-2
ISBN (hc) 978-1-7364520-1-1
ISBN (eb) 978-1-7364520-0-4

Printed in the USA First Edition

Dedication

To you, the Reader,

A blessing from a father to his child...

"May the Beloved of The Lord dwell in safety by Him; He shields and covers him all the day long, and he dwells between His shoulders."
Deuteronomy 33:12

...you are the Beloved.

Contents

Preface

Do you believe that your awareness of the ever-present nearness and goodness of God can change everything?

From the beginning of time, God, the Creator, wanted companionship. His Spirit hovered above the formless, emptiness of the earth. Everything was still, dark, and quiet until He began to speak. His words were like atom bombs of energy that created space and everything in it! The sun, moon, and stars were set into place by His words alone! His WORDS were the genesis of every created thing and He said it was "good."

On the final day of creation, He created mankind, male and female, in His image and He blessed them, as He took in all that He made, He said it "was very good." He created a garden where He could walk with them in the cool of the day. That is until Adam and Eve had to leave the oasis that God had built for them. Even then, God blessed them. From that moment on, the reconciliation plan of "Love" was set into motion. Jesus became flesh so that we could be restored as The Beloved of The Lord, and walk in the fullness of The Blessing that He spoke over creation.

Generation after generation have come and gone since the first days of creation. Life can be hard. Things happen that are out of our control and we become bitter, resentful, and offended. The pain of living with the choices of generations past has left its mark and stolen the blessing and the authority that was always intended for The Heirs of The Throne of God.

Your awareness of that blessing can bring reconciliation and restoration to your family tree all the way back to your genesis (or beginning) in an instant! It's as quick as putting on a pair of glasses.

The Strongman had his claws in everyone's business. It was a generational thing that was evidenced by the dark glasses that dimmed the wearers' vision. It was as if the glasses tinted everything with fear.

Part One

The Strongman Rules

The Strongman ruled in The Town of Silence and The Family of Betrayal was quite content with their "keeper." They didn't challenge him, and he left them alone, or so they thought. Most every business and family in town had been covertly infiltrated by at least one of The Strongman's agents. In truth, The Strongman had his claws in everyone's business. It was a generational thing that was evidenced by the dark glasses that dimmed the wearers' vision. It was as if the glasses tinted everything with fear. The Town of Silence, a place where everyone knew, yet no one talked. It could be Anytown, USA. Just as, The Betrayal Family could be any family. And since we're being honest, Despair, the Betrayal's daughter, could be any one of us at any given time.

Mr. and Mrs. Betrayal, Deceit and Martyr, were perfectly suited for each other. Deceit had another life, one full of secrets. Martyr, deep down, flourished in The Family of Suffering because she felt no responsibility for the situation before her. You see, she was pregnant and did not want to be! Her second baby was not conceived in love like the first daughter, but in violence. The arrival of a baby is supposed to be a joyous thing. Not this baby! This baby brings pain formed memories, too many to recall, and with them illness, and a lifetime of suffering and despair. She will be a flesh and blood reminder of the betrayal and shame that Martyr was now carrying. No, this baby would not be joyously celebrated but reviled for all time. She will be named Despair, for that is what she brings. She is born into The Family of Betrayal, and she will grow up in The Town of Silence.

Tiny towns are funny places. The web of interconnectedness can be a comfort or a prison depending on which side of town you live in, who your family is or isn't, and whether you live a perfect life according to the people in charge. The comparisons were crushing and once labeled by The Town, inhabitants are stuck. Have you ever tried to peel a label off something and you could never get the sticky bits off? That's what it felt like trying to grow up in The Town of Silence.

The Betrayal Family lived large and loud. According to Deceit, outside rules were mere suggestions to choose which ones he wanted to follow. Inside rules were an altogether different matter, you follow them, or you suffer. PERIOD. To defy Deceit's rules was an invitation to a beating. Most of the time the marks from the battering were well concealed and no one outside the four walls of their house would be any the wiser. Except for the time when Despair couldn't walk without limping. She skipped school, so as not to attract undue attention from anyone who would ask questions.

> Growing up in
> The Town of Silence was
> like living in a broken
> washing machine...

Growing up in The Town of Silence was like living in a broken washing machine, you think that you've chosen the "gentle/delicate" cycle but the only one that ever works is the "heavy duty/soiled" cycle. Just when you think you know how to handle the dirt in your life, you get tossed into a tub that pours water on top of you, rotates you mercilessly, then spins you until you don't know which way is up! A perfect description of what it felt like to grow up in The Town of Silence.

To rightly tell this story, I must give you a glimpse into The Frozen Years before Despair came to be known as Hope. I call them The Frozen Years because it's as if the early days had been isolated, held in suspended animation, just waiting for the full riches of complete understanding, so that she could know the mystery that was hidden for her to find.[6] The Frozen Years seemed to trap her, but in the end, they only served as a journey to transform her into Hope, preparing her for her Beloved.

Happily, Ever After?

Deceit had betrayed Martyr again and her children were witnesses to a cycle that was not about to end there. A cycle of abuses that were always somehow justified and then, as if by some sort of magic, disappeared. However, neither was true, they were not forgiven or forgotten.

Martyr was on the run, dragging Success, Oblivious, and Despair out into the cold dark night. Martyr's family, The Sufferings, had come to her rescue yet again. They ran many times before, so this vanishing act was nothing new to Despair and her sisters. Being just children, they did not know what Deceit's betrayal had been. They just knew that it was very mysterious and horrible. The strangest element of this exodus was that they were running from Deceit when they were used to running *with* him, and this fact was not lost on Martyr's young daughters.

Deceit had a habit, you see, of running from the right and just things of life. He and his brother Entitlement were infamous in The Town of Silence, for Betrayal was their father.

Entitlement, however, who had a seemingly chance encounter with a young teacher who appeared to be Wisdom personified, would eventually be instrumental in altering the course of Despair's life. But not tonight.

This night was distinctly darker than the night before. Maybe it was the urgency that hung in the air like a smothering, utterly black cloud. They had to work as quickly as possible if the truck was to be loaded and gone before Deceit returned home. Martyr's brothers, Scorn and Sympathy, helped carry out the beds and boxes of clothing, one after the other. The truck was filling up fast. The house was left with basic furniture and pictures still hanging on the walls, but it was void of life and noticeably empty. Blankets and pillows were stuffed into a reliable little car leaving enough room for Martyr and Oblivious. Success would ride in the cab of the

> Despair fell fast asleep in Sympathy's arms in what could easily have been described as a prison.

moving truck with her Uncle Scorn. There was scarcely enough space in the very back of the moving truck, on top of a table, for Despair and her other Uncle Sympathy, who knew the secret that surrounded this little golden-haired girl.

It was just past midnight when the door rumbled into place, the latch was secured, and they were engulfed in the cold darkness as they left.

Surprisingly Despair fell fast asleep in Sympathy's arms in what could easily have been described as a prison. Neither one could see the heavenly agents that were surrounding them, yet concealed in the darkness.

About four hours had passed when the small caravan of refugees arrived at The Suffering's house hundreds of miles from The Town of Silence. Still shrouded in darkness, they made their way inside to warm blankets and silent hugs from a sleepy Aunt Bliss. None of The Sufferings had ever approved of Martyr's choice of a husband. Now they had their proof. He was just a sinner from the bloodline of Betrayal. They all were.

When morning finally came, a falsely repentant Deceit was already trying to find his family. Martyr was predictable, so he knew where they would be, back in the nest of The Sufferings. He was right. Now he had to persuade Scorn and Sympathy to let him wiggle back into Martyr's good graces. It wouldn't be easy, but Deceit was an expert in these matters. It took him a great deal of time and some fast-talking. Now he was no longer hundreds of miles away but on Scorn's front porch. Suffering had united them once again. The Strongman's face twisted into a repulsive, snarly grin as he savored the moment.

Adventures Galore!

Oh, the many adventures of Despair. Although during most of these early years, she didn't know that her life was far from "Ideal," a place where Despair wanted to live. She'd heard that it was always warm and satisfying there. Not at all like the barren and frigid place that held Despair captive. What did she know? She was just a kid. She couldn't see it as a kid, but her heart longed for "Ideal."

> Despair was not alone in her little world;
> she had two sisters,
> Success and Oblivious.

Despair was not alone in her little world; she had two beautiful sisters, Success and Oblivious. Success, the eldest sister, was smart and eloquent. Her chestnut hair matched her rich dancing eyes.

Those eyes sparkled with dreams that she held so close as not to lose sight of them. She was petite and soft-spoken; she learned early on that there was power and strength in silence — not at all like Despair. Despair was like a storm, loud and boisterous, with flaming hair that matched her personality, fiery and intense. There was a "come what may" air about her. She was fearless, courageous, and unstoppable. Her hazel eyes reflected her moods and flickered and flashed when she laughed, completely unaware that she was despised for being joyful while living in The Town of Silence. Oblivious, the youngest, was entirely a sight to behold. She always laughed with effortless abandon even in dire situations! Her eyes were the color of the sky on a cloudless day, and her long blonde hair framed her face like a halo of golden sunshine. She was special. Despair was nothing like Oblivious.

Being the middle child of three daughters wasn't easy, Despair was often reminded that she was "stubborn and defiant." She was encouraged to "be more like Success" or to "let things roll, like Oblivious." Despair came to believe the lie that she was "too much" and "not enough" simultaneously, and she eventually became what her name described her to be. Despair.

These were The Frozen Years.

To hide the truths of his life, Deceit spirited his family away from his lies and accusers to the frozen wilderness on the edge of civilization. He was confident that no one would find him there. No one except The Strongman, for there was still a game to play.

Having been torn away from her family, The Sufferings, and being careful to conceal all her displeasure, Martyr put on her best brave face as she followed Deceit into the frozen tundra. Days turned into months, months into years! Things were about to change forever in ways she couldn't possibly imagine.

Escaping to Freedom!

Shortly after her eighteenth birthday, Success,

Despair's older sister, escaped the influence of Deceit and the frozen wilderness only to find herself a world away in the desert. Even though she was free, the distance felt like a lonely prison. Was this what she had dreamed of all along? Was this freedom? Someone would have to pay for her breach, for no one defies The Strongman without suffering. The Strongman had a way of getting his "pound of flesh" when a breach happened, and Success paid dearly for pursuing her dreams. She was cut off from family, like an orphan, and every success she achieved was celebrated on her own. To call it "bittersweet" was an understatement and it affected her deeply. This "bitter suffering" was just part of The Strongman's "pound of flesh."

> Despair had heard about the Savior. Martyr was often quoting things He had said or written.

Despair had also tried to escape from being Deceit's daughter by setting out on a journey for higher knowledge and truth. However, she was not free from the wrath that The Strongman had in store for her. Pride had become Despair's newest companion. Pride had her own sisters, Distortion, Defiance, and Suicide, who masqueraded as Relief. Pride was a sneaky trick that always worked for The Strongman, yet it was another subtle "pound of flesh" payment.

The National Suicide Prevention Lifeline provides free and confidential emotional support to people in suicidal crisis or emotional distress 24 hours a day, 7 days a week, across the United States. Call the Lifeline at 1-800-273-8255.

Oblivious, Despair's younger sister had a way of finding something to laugh about regularly. It was as if she were blissfully unaware of the constant turmoil around her. Bliss and Beauty helped Oblivious in ways that Despair could only dream of, and she envied the ease that her sister walked in so effortlessly. The Strongman had no foothold in Oblivious, so he left her alone.

Despair had heard about The Savior. Martyr was often quoting things He had said or written. He didn't seem like much of a savior, though, for Martyr seemed to be endlessly suffering. There was no joy in her eyes, no song in her heart. Wasn't the definition of a savior "one who delivers or rescues"? Who was this savior that Martyr spoke of often?

Whoever he was, Despair was not interested in knowing him. For the life Martyr lived was a dismal and seemingly hopeless existence as far as Despair could tell. There was no room for Martyr's kind of savior.

Despair would have to be her own savior. So, the quest began:

> The search for perfection.
>
> The longing to be loved.
>
> The reality of her sad life.
>
> Sick at heart and in constant disappointment.
>
> The hopelessness of life.
>
> The promise of freedom in death.
>
> The plan...Relief.

Relief versus Love

She remembered hearing "stories" about Jesus from Entitlement and Martyr. Saying that He was a "friend"[15] who never leaves or abandons, and she really liked that idea. Her reality was that she didn't have many "real friends," mostly people in her life who had to be there because they were family. Despair wanted "real friends" who last the test of time and stick around when life gets messy, and boy did she have a messy life! As a kid, Despair did exactly what she was told to do so that Jesus would be her friend. They said that she needed to "walk the Roman Road," whatever that was, and to say "The Sinner's Prayer."[16] So she did. She asked Jesus to forgive her and to live in her heart. That made people around her very happy, it seemed, but her life really didn't change that much. She wondered if she was an unchangeable sinner deep down in her tiny human heart.

> Years blurred into one another and she stumbled upon some new "friends," "Distortion" and "Defiance."

As time went on, the mess Despair lived in seemed to overtake her, and she forgot about this idea of "Jesus is my friend." Years blurred into one another, and she stumbled upon some new "friends," named "Distortion" and "Defiance." They were cold and frigid, utterly void of the love that Despair so desperately desired.

Nothing went right for Despair. It seemed as if everything in all of existence was set against her. She wasn't small enough, smart enough, or pretty enough. Despair simply wasn't enough of anything, really. She was a disappointment to everyone. Despair believed that she'd never be satisfied because her expectations were just too high. Somehow Despair had mastered the art of being both "too much and not enough" simultaneously. At least that's what she learned from her ever-present "friend" Distortion.

Her other new "friend" Defiance was all kinds of sassy! Defiance told her that people were just jealous and wished that they could be as care-free as Despair! I mean really, it seemed that nothing could hurt Despair's feelings! Call her fat, no big deal. Say that she's "nothing compared to her beautiful sisters" — whatever. Despair learned from Defiance how to be stone-cold while locking her emotions up in a prison of ice. Defiance taught her how to protect herself. Little did she know that Defiance and Distortion were simply setting her up for an appointment with "Relief."

Relief had a game plan of his own. He was really The Strongman in a clever disguise. Desperate humans were easy to deceive with words that were just close enough to the truth. Relief fancied himself to be a master manipulator and knew how to use his not so subtle companions, Defiance and Distortion, to wear people down and talk them into an unthinkable end, suicide. He enjoyed the game of twisting realities and sprinkling in half-truths to gain their trust and then serve up the right amount of offense to make people hate each other. His challenge was not to let the stupid humans know that they were being played, like a sick chess game where everyone loses. Mind you; everyone loses at this game except The Strongman.

The rules of the game went something like this, make them miserable until you're able to convince the sniveling fools that Relief will help them and everyone around them by taking away "the problem." He convinces you that you are the problem, and the solution is to stop living.

"Suicide. It's actually the kindest thing you can do for the people that you love because you are going to take your problem with you when you go." That is The Strongman's lie, and he smoothly delivered it with a forked-tongue.

You see, there is one rule that The Strongman cannot break. He cannot take an Heir to The Throne's life. He's simply not that powerful; he must convince them to kill themselves. Defiance, Distortion, and Relief are Suicide incognito, which are also slaves in The Strongman's chess game.

The National Suicide Prevention Lifeline provides free and confidential emotional support to people in suicidal crisis or emotional distress 24 hours a day, 7 days a week, across the United States. Call the Lifeline at 1-800-273-8255.

The funny thing is that The Strongman has a sickness of his own – it's called Pride. Pride doesn't discriminate. It infects any willing vessel that gives attention to it. Pride causes its sufferers to believe their own press that goes something like this, "I am untouchable, unquestionable, uncorrectable, unchallengeable, and I am above the rules of Love." The problem with Pride is that it always brings a destructive fall.

The second sickness that plagues The Strongman is a solid case of amnesia. He always forgets his losses when he plays against Love, because Love always wins. Always!

Despair was miserably unaware of Love's power. The prize for Relief's game would be her life. Three rounds were played, Love won all three.

The Strongman had a way of attacking the young. He has been particularly successful at talking the young 13-year-old girls out of their lives. They are easy to convince that their lives are over if

> The Strongman had a way of attacking the young. He is particularly successful at talking 13-year-old girls out of their lives.

he could isolate them and feed them a steady stream of disinformation.

Depression. Isolation in the long dark winter. Powerlessness because she's just a kid. Let the games begin.

Round One. Despair couldn't handle the constant fighting in her household. If Deceit and Martyr weren't fighting over the lack of money, they were fighting with Despair over her grades. She wasn't trying hard enough, after all being smart is all that she had going for her, it certainly wasn't her beauty that would bring her advancement.

Despair hoped that she wouldn't wake up. She hoped that she was tangled enough and that her ability to breath would be cut off. She was unknowingly listening to the lies of Relief's twisted game. As her breathing shallowed and her vision went black, Relief smirked with a sick satisfaction.

As Love would have it, sometime after Despair blacked out, Love crossed the invisible barrier of the natural world and caused her to move ever so slightly. Just enough air entered her lungs and her brain responded with its innate response—inhale-exhale, inhale-exhale. Despair would live. First round, Love – 1, Relief- 0. Love didn't falter in His stance as Relief shifted and consulted The Strongman's rules for the game while setting up for the next round.

Round Two. No one knew that Despair had intended never to wake up that day. But she did. Relief whispered into her ear, "Here's to another day of being a disappointment." Despair wilted. It was as if she'd been frostbitten and she couldn't actually feel her feelings anymore. The pain inside became like a gnawing worm that invaded her thoughts, *however* Despair could find Relief would be an acceptable plan for her weary heart. Despair had no idea that these aching thoughts were not her own so she welcomed them.

Despair and her sister Oblivious walked home daily along a treacherous stretch of highway. The busy road was flanked with high banks of snow and one misstep at just the precise moment would provide enough impact to end her misery in an instant. It will look like an accident; it'd be better for her family if they thought it was an accident. The plan was set. "Tomorrow. I'll do it tomorrow." Despair echoed what Relief hissed into her ear. "Another tense night and it'll be done; I won't contribute to the problems anymore." But Love had a plan for tomorrow too.

Despair made sure that Oblivious had gone on ahead of her so she wouldn't see "the accident." The wind was gusting, it would assist her "slipping into traffic." Despair's eyes stung with tears as she hoped that it wouldn't hurt too badly. "Even if it did, it wouldn't even come close to the emotional pain that you cause your family daily, the relief will be worth it. Just a few more steps." Relief keeping up his constant drip of grotesque "encouragement."

Just then Oblivious whipped her head around and called out to Despair, saying, "I don't know what I'd do without you!" Neither girl could see that they had stepped into a gap in time and space! It was like a pocket of pure light, not a speck of darkness existed, and it was saturated with Love's Presence! In this pocketlike atmosphere, Love spoke directly THROUGH Oblivious and His words went straight to Despair's heart! She was instantly GRIPPED by Love Himself and her foot didn't slip at the "chosen spot"! Instant tears gushed from Despair's eyes as she heard "Love's word through her sister's voice" and in that moment, Round Two was over! Despair lived, again. Love smiled. They continued their walk home along the snow-covered highway. Despair's pain continued, but Love had a plan.

> Just then Oblivious whipped her head around and called out to Despair, saying, "I don't know what I'd do without you."

Round Two, Love - 2, Relief - still 0.

Relentless, The Strongman plotted Round Three. The Person of Love is known by many names. Despair's Uncle Entitlement had met Love as a "young teacher" and called her Wisdom. Uncle Entitlement had an encounter with Wisdom that altered him. Entitlement was renamed Confidence and it was time for Despair to be properly introduced. It was quite the tale that Despair's Uncle told her about having been transformed by this "young teacher"—Wisdom personified. Despair, still frostbitten in heart, listened to her Uncle's amazing story with bitter ears. Nothing. She heard nothing and felt nothing, she was numb. Her heart had succumbed to the subzero temperatures that had also claimed her emotions. All Despair wanted was a hot shower to warm her.

Relief came again trying to win this time with a razor in the shower. Yet again, Love prevailed. This time Love intervened with a constant pounding on the bathroom door by those who were next in line for the shower! The pounding was accompanied by declarations of "you're so selfish" and "you're using all of the hot water!" Despair sobbed with bitter tears razor in hand. "I hate you." she said beneath her breath, knowing full well that her escape wouldn't be coming tonight! Despair reluctantly turned off the hot water and scraped the tears from her face with a scratchy towel. Love was standing on the other side of the bathroom door with the most tender look of compassion on His face and tears in His eyes. "I love you Despair. I can't wait to meet you tomorrow," He said.

Love always wins. Love - 3, Relief - 0. Game over.

> Eventually Love would show her the reality of Relief being nothing more than suicide deceptively veiled as a temporary "solution" with an eternal consequence.

Despair would know very soon that her "Friend," Jesus, The Person of Love, was always there, that He never left her or abandoned her. Eventually Love would show her the reality of Relief being nothing more than Suicide deceptively veiled as a temporary "solution" with an Eternal consequence.

The National Suicide Prevention Lifeline provides free and confidential emotional support to people in suicidal crisis or emotional distress 24 hours a day, 7 days a week, across the United States. Call the Lifeline at 1-800-273-8255.

A Mirage in the Land of Ideal?

Divine appointment set; this would be no ordinary day. Having survived her latest attempt to find Relief, Despair realized she must be searching for something. Or was she searching for someone? She didn't know the answer. But the answer found her quickly in the form of a question. It was delivered by a "Mirage" sent from the Land of Ideal!

Despair found herself in a most beautiful meadow with green grass and wildflowers as far as her eyes could see. It was absolutely Ideal.

> "Which way will you go? You must choose," The Source of Light spoke.

Curiously, the warmth she was experiencing wasn't coming from the sky. It was coming from the massive figure full of light standing beside her! She wondered, "Is this real?"

"Which way will you go? You must choose," The Source of Light spoke.

Every fiber of her being quivered with the knowledge of whose company she was sharing; it was no mirage! She remembered being told that every person with breath in their lungs had a "God-shaped hole in them that could only be filled with God Himself." She thought it was just a stupid, manipulative saying. However, right there at that moment, Despair *knew* she had a "God-shaped hole," and her solution to satisfy the void in her life was standing right beside her! She couldn't explain HOW she knew – she just KNEW!

Despair was standing in the presence of I AM! The, I AM! The Father of the Savior! And he was talking to her! The scent of roses laced the air, warmed by the radiant heat that emanated from the Being standing beside her. His light was warmer and brighter than any sunny day Despair had ever felt or seen. What Despair didn't know was that I AM is The Source of Light!

"God is light, and there is no darkness in him at all." **1 John 1:5, NLT**

Was this real? The cool grass under her feet felt real, and she felt more alive than ever before. It had to be real! The firm yet gentle hand of I AM held Despair ever so lovingly. She'd never felt love from a simple touch before. To be honest, she'd never felt love this unconditional before. "Love with strings," Despair was well acquainted with, but this was exciting and filled with compassion. She never wanted to let go of his hand for fear that she would never feel the rapture of this moment again. Standing at a fork in the path they'd been walking along, I AM started speaking again. She could feel the air tremble as his words fell to her ears.

"You must choose." I AM repeated.

Both paths in the fork seemed to be lined with identical green blades of grass, no stones to trip and stumble over, each seemingly as safe as the other. Despair thoughtlessly pointed in the direction that she chose to travel, forgetting the emptiness that had been consumed as they walked along.

"That is not The Way. I cannot go there with you." I AM spoke in reply to her choice.

But Despair was no stranger to being alone, and Defiance reminded her that she was not afraid to stand by her chosen path. I AM turned His head for a moment, she released His hand, and with her first step, her heart began to plummet. Pride stopped her from turning and running headlong back into I AM's arms. Pride had been a longtime companion through many of Despair's "adventures." With each step she took, the colors that she had previously reveled in seemed to fade, and the warmth that caressed her skin silently slipped away. The path that had once been so serene began to reveal its well concealed thorns. Forty painful steps were taken before Despair finally came to her end, throwing herself to the rocky ground. Her body wracking with sobs and bitter tears falling from her eyes, the realization that she was repeating the cycle she'd learned from her family, seized her heart! Pride wailed tortuously and then vanished into thin air as Despair wept."

> I AM turned His head for a moment, she released His hand, and with her first step, her heart began to plummet.

"I MUST GO BACK! I'd rather die than stay on this path and become the very thing that I've always hated." She cried, unaware if she was actually speaking. The moment that Despair turned around, it seemed as if time stood still. I AM was directly in front of her with His hands outstretched! "I've been behind you all along, my dear. But I had to wait for you to turn back to me." He spoke.

"Do we have to go back?" whispered Despair, who was willing to confront her wrong choice if it meant she could stay in the presence of I AM. "No, we can go on from here," I AM answered.

Trembling, Despair took his outstretched hand in her own, and instantly she found what she'd been longing for her entire life. Rapturous joy exploded and consumed the void in her heart with the realization that she made the most important decision of her whole life. She would never forget the words that he spoke next, for they felt like a mighty rushing wind, "I would like you to meet my son, The Savior – The Person of Love."

The Savior

The Savior was not at all as Despair pictured Him.
All that she'd ever heard about him had come through the filter of
Martyr; he'd never rescued Martyr from suffering or answered her
prayers, so it seemed to Despair that he would be a small and weak
kind of Being. He had the form of a man but was different. There was
a passionate intensity in his eyes that seemed to look directly into
Despair's heart. She couldn't tear herself away from His gaze. He
knew everything. Instantly her heart was laid bare before him. Yet
there he stood. He didn't run. He didn't turn away with shame and
disappointment in his gaze. Unable to stand any longer, Despair
crumbled at His feet, weeping, not able to say a word. The Savior
raised his hands and tenderly placed them on top of her head. He
spoke her name, and Despair felt as if something wet was pouring
over her. It was warm and smelled intoxicatingly sweet, and her hand
seemed to float up to the crown of her head. Her fingers brushed the
Savior's hands and were met with a thick, sticky substance. She
withdrew her hand to the level of her eyes, and for a moment, terror

struck her heart. Her sins had finally required its payment. She would die today. Blood was pouring onto her head and over her shoulders from gushing wounds in the Savior's hands and wrists. Again, time stood still as Despair realized she was now kneeling in a pool of blood, not her blood, but the Savior's powerful, innocent, spotless blood. She could see every hateful, spiteful thing that she had ever said and done in its reflection. As she sat paralyzed by the reality of her actions being consumed and cleansed by innocent blood, a strange calm settled over her heart.

> Surrendered and yielded, Despair broke the deafening silence. "I am Your's," she whispered...

Surrendered and yielded, Despair broke the deafening silence. "I am Your's," she whispered, "if you'll have me." "I will." replied The Savior, who went on to say, "Walk with me, and let me show you how I've always loved you."

Now the real journey began, one that took her through time and space. Like a trapped little bird that finally finds freedom, Despair opened her mouth and out flew a melody whose name was Extreme

Hope! She was a new creation.

Hope learned what happened on that fateful day when she met Jesus, The Savior. Not only was she instantly and completely forgiven, but she also received the extraordinary gift of grace.

Part Two

Between Then and Now

Hope learned what happened on that fateful day when she met Jesus, The Savior. Not only was she instantly and completely forgiven, but she also received the extraordinary gift of grace. Grace, a hidden power that allowed her to do what she could not do before! Hope learned how to forgive and truly love, and it started with learning to love herself! She previously hated her life and everything about it! She wasn't born into a happy family. After all, her family's name was Betrayal. Now, Hope saw everything differently after she met The Savior named Jesus in a puddle of blood.

> "Grace," a hidden power, that allowed her to do what she could not do before.

Hope couldn't tell you how that grace worked. She just knew that it did. The Betrayal Family was stuck in a place of not knowing what they didn't know, which is the nature of deception, those caught in its trap don't know what they don't know. Hope learned how to "hope against all hope."[17] It didn't make sense to her natural mind, but she KNEW how to stand in belief and simply love, even though she didn't like what her natural eyes could see. Somehow her vision had been affected when she knelt in that red puddle.

Hope learned that I AM loved her childlike offerings; the simpler, the better. Hope discovered that partnering with I AM while she waited for unseen things to be pulled into reality required her to surrender her desire to understand it all. Which was quite

> Hope learned that
> I AM loved her
> child-like offerings, the
> simpler the better.

an elegant offering that even the wisest often couldn't understand. How is the surrender of your understanding wise? It was actually quite simple; surrendering her need to understand put her precisely in a posture of trusting I AM, also known as The Author of Hope. It was an act of her will to step into faith.[4]

Hope, however, knew that since I AM collided with Despair in a most unimaginable fashion and restored her to the Hope that she was always created to be, I AM could do the same thing for her family! Hope now lived in the absolute expectation of the goodness of I AM to show up and show off, in astonishing ways! Despair had indeed been transformed into Hope. She knew the radical transformation she'd experienced and wanted it for everyone, including her family.

The Redefining Years

The marriage of Hope and Prince Charming some 20 plus years ago, established The Beloved Family and this union completely redefined both of their stories. The Beloved's lived in The City of Trees.[11] It was a magical place full of choices and unlimited possibilities, promises made and kept, and vibrant colors of every hue were seen upon its citizens. A stark difference from The Town of Silence, the place that seemed to be forever holding its residents captive in an eternal deep-freeze of sorts, eyes open but never really seeing.

Their life together was nothing short of miraculous, and Hope's heart was redefined as a result. Awareness of the seeds of Truth that had been planted long before burst forth as if they had seen a great light[10], and for the first time, she and her Beloved Prince Charming were living powerful and FREE!

Many seasons had come and gone. Summer, Spring, Winter, and Fall, each one a pleasure to behold. Hope and Prince Charming had built a beautiful family while living out loud the mystery of The One who holds all things together. [6 & 7] Their three children had grown strong and confident in the atmosphere of wisdom and knowledge they lived in at home. They learned that they were powerful and could choose the lives that they wanted to live throughout their days. They discovered that they were not victims of circumstance. Even if things were "out of their control," they always got to choose how they were going to respond. These were lessons straight from the genesis of Time itself. They learned them from Jesus

> They learned that they were powerful and could choose the lives they wanted to live throughout their days.

– The Son, who is the replica of God Himself. [9]

The Beloved's learned that both "success" and "failure" could deliver invaluable wisdom. Wisdom, however, is never "free," there is always a cost. You could pay for it first hand, which was usually a price far more than you'd like to pay, OR you could gain wisdom by learning from those around you who've already learned "the hard way."[13] Either way you choose to learn, wisdom is gained. Success can be achieved, and Failure is never failure unless you fail to learn.

> ...failure is never failure, unless you fail to learn.

Despair paid the price for wisdom firsthand and was transformed into Hope by the process. She was thankful, even though the transformation had not been an easy one.

Her metamorphosis often reminded Hope of the journey that a caterpillar must endure while surrendering to the process of becoming a butterfly. The caterpillar starts out being held captive by gravity and endlessly consuming the leaves of whatever tree they find themselves in at any given moment. That is until they form a cocoon and settle into the uncomfortable confines of their hot new space. It's as if the heat reduces every bit of their bodies into a mushy gooey mess until the restructuring begins. The formerly constricted body gives way to a beautiful pair of glassy wings that are unseen because the increasingly fragile cocoon is protecting them. At just the right moment, the butterfly struggles to break free from her current prison only to discover that it wasn't a prison at all! It was an incubator! Hope loved the visual idea of a caterpillar's transformation into a butterfly! It gave wisdom that would serve her well in the days ahead.

Despair's transformation into Hope was necessary for her to conquer the Land of Extreme. Hope would be forever marked by the journey that lay ahead, but The Savior, her Defender, was ready. The Strongman wanted Hope to forfeit The Blessing by recapturing Despair and taking her back into bondage, so he had to make her question her transformation. He'd been quiet for a season, but he planned to remind this stupid girl of her years of Suffering. Memories can be powerful prisons if visited often enough, mused The Strongman. The one thing that he didn't anticipate was that Hope would now be journeying with The Savior back into The Land of Extreme Suffering.

The Land of Extreme?

Hand in hand with The Savior, Hope watched memories bend and fold over on themselves. Time-shifted, and she found herself in "The Land of Extreme Hope." Was her transformation even real? Hope, I mean. Is "Hope" even a "thing"?

The Land of Extreme Hope seemed like this intangible faraway place that was always out of reach for her as Despair. Was Extreme Hope a place at all? Is it possible that Extreme Hope was just an idea, a figment of her over-active imagination?

"I hope this happens." "I hope that happens." "We can only hope." These are common wishful thoughts, deferred hopes of everyday people that fall from their mouths like raindrops from the sky, watering the dry landscape with heartsick disappointment.[12]

Overcast and gloomy. Drip. Drip. Drip. Honestly, hope, REAL HOPE, isn't a reality that most "regular people" can grasp, let alone "Extreme Hope." What even IS that?!!

"When hope's dream seems to drag on and on, the delay can be depressing. But when at last your dream comes true, life's sweetness, like a tree of life, will satisfy your soul." **Proverbs 13:12**

A friend of The Savior had written those words. History remembers him as "Solomon," and his house was that of a king!

Even when Hope was lost in Despair, she didn't want a palace, she dreamt of a dream home in her heart. She always wanted a house built in the trees like a bird's nest! The vantage point from high above the realities of life's details felt like HOPE to her. Alas, dreams that drag on and on never materializing far below the realm of possibility, when she was Despair, she lived in that land daily, that is, until now.

Despair flew on the wings of possibility to a land far away to share the heart song that she always sang when alone. Since meeting The

Savior, it seemed that she was always singing. Her song sounded different now, she couldn't put her finger on it, she just knew that "different was good."

"Hallelujah. Hallelujah. The storm is passing over. Hallelujah." Her song was "Extreme" considering her name. But "Extreme" was good, nonetheless.

The definition of despair is an utter loss of hope and/or a cause of hopelessness. Martyr told her once, "I named you after my enemy so that I could always remember my hatred." Memory number one landed out of nowhere!

At that moment, it took Despair only a fraction of a second to discover that she was wearing a marvelous pair of glasses, through which she could see that she wasn't the enemy that Martyr hated! After 40 years of their tormented relationship, everything suddenly made sense! Martyr hated her circumstance and just didn't have the tools to deal with this "situation" in the form of a baby! With surprising tenderness Despair said, "Mom, I'm not the woman you hated. I'm not her. I'm so sorry that you've carried that for all of these years." The conversation continued but it was if Martyr's words were a dull buzz in Despair's ears. All she could hear was the heartbeat of understanding pulsing through her entire body. Despair finally understood her mother's "why," the reason *why* she did all the things she'd done! The awareness of it left her speechless.

Despair pulled the glasses from her eyes, and to her delight was introduced to a new friend at that moment. Compassion, a friend of The Savior's, was standing beside her, holding a most extraordinary pair of matching pink glasses that shifted and bent the light ever so slightly. When she looked through Compassion's glasses, everything changed. The change was EXTREME!

Anything "extreme" exceeds the ordinary, usual, or expected, which seemed a perfectly fitting way to describe Despair. She WAS "extreme." There didn't seem to be anything "that exceeded the ordinary, usual, or unexpected" about her. Or so she thought! She later discovered that through the new "pink lenses," she was extraordinary. She was quite unusual in a good way, as she always occupied unexpected territory with the greatest of ease. It had to be because of the awareness of her newfound companion, Compassion, who was the only common denominator in her new perspective.

The Strongman was about to explode! Despair isn't supposed to see Compassion! She was supposed to see Suffering! Extreme Suffering! Compassion caused his plans to backfire, and all she could

> She later discovered that through the new "pink lenses," she was extraordinary

see was Extreme Hope! Still The Strongman wasn't ready to let go of Despair.

Awareness Happens!

The Strongman was suddenly weak and he realized that he lost control of the situation before him. Compassion was running the show now.

There were still times and places, filled with memories, to visit. However, with her newfound awareness, the name "Despair" didn't seem to "fit" anymore. Even so, she was very fidgety as if she knew something BIG was about to happen. They say that "time will tell," and yet, as Despair could determine, it's not time that tells. It's an awareness that changes everything.

Despair was not really sure when her awareness happened. When had she become aware? She finally realized she'd been judging her family the entire time with the same condemning eyes that she'd always thought were condemning her! It was like a bomb went off in her heart while awareness instantly flooded every crack and crevice! She'd been sitting in judgment against her family, which condemned them to stay in Suffering!

A great revelation came to Despair. "I SEE! It was never me that Martyr hated! Martyr hated the circumstance that she felt powerless in, and she simply didn't know how to handle it! I can't even imagine how conflicted her feelings must have been when she laid eyes on me. I know she loved me; she just didn't know how to show it." A tear silently slid down her cheek as she mused aloud. "I'm so sorry Martyr. I'm so sorry that our lives together were so hard. I wish I had known this sooner. I can only imagine how different our relationship could have been."

Again, Despair felt the familiar warmth of being held by I AM. Safe. Known. Peaceful. Astonished. Loved. The awareness of I AM's nearness affected her this way, and she felt goosebumps on her cheeks. It's as if He'd lovingly brushed her with His goodness.

"I'm so sorry, Mom. I now see that you really did the best that you could. I forgive you," Despair whispered. Those last three words, "I forgive you." caused the atmosphere to shift physically! The leaves on the massive trees responded and gently fluttered, bearing witness to her words.

What was the sound that had just flown out of her mouth? Hope?!? Yes, HOPE! She remembered that sound and she liked it very much, it felt EXTREME and perfect! She remembered that the definition of extreme is exceeding the ordinary, usual, or expected. She identified with those words in an entirely different way now.

Previously "EXTREME" felt like defiance. Defiance was EXCITING because it made her feel alive, if only temporarily. Suddenly she was no longer Despair from The Town of Silence. No longer simply surviving as a defiant little girl. No longer "impossible." Just then, in that very moment of awareness, "Despair" disappeared into a dull puff of smoke that was carried away by the breeze. The woman who remained was a shiny, yet feisty, "Hope" who saw everything through the eyes of possibility! Her "hope" had become a reality, and she now lived in The City of Trees!

> Awareness changes everything!

Awareness changes everything, including The Strongman. He trembled, as awareness seemed to tangibly flicker across his body as if his very form had been altered – weakened and a bit shrunken. Extreme horror is a fitting description of his face. She was waking up and waking up to a reality that was more real than she could've possibly imagined. Despair had come alive to her newfound name of Hope. The dance of deception would have to get much more skilled. More than just the simple two-step that The Strongman had become fond of years past. Little Miss "Hope" could get accustomed to her expanded existence from her elevated position in The City of Trees if he was not careful.

The Strongman thought it's time for a walk down, "memory lane." That always worked. Revisit the frozen past on the newly encouraged and emboldened Escapee. She would stumble quickly and cave easily. Or so he thought.

Just then, The Strongman realized that he wasn't alone in his observation of the departure of "Despair" and the revealing of "Hope." Compassion?!! What was HE doing here?!! His presence wasn't part of the plan! He had no idea that Compassion would be along for every journey from now on. Not only that, Compassion always had those blasted glasses for "Hope" to wear, the sparkly pink ones that seemed to shift and bend everything that "Despair" saw into an entirely new perspective. The Strongman was nauseated just thinking about those darn glasses!

"I refuse to call her by another name except for Despair." He whispered aloud. "I hate you." Compassion quickly replied, "I love you." The Strongman seemed to grimace and melt a little. He silently hoped that Compassion couldn't see how effective those three little words were, growling, "Let's get on with this."

All the while, "Hope" was simply unaware of the struggle taking place for her attention and awareness. She was too thrilled with her new name and how it made her feel! She had often heard the cloying term of endearment, "I love you to death!" She never really understood it, mostly because it just didn't sound all that appealing. Now, THIS feeling of HOPE is what being "loved to life" felt like for everyone! She WANTED this kind of Love in her life from now on!!

Compassion silently observed, taking notes.

A Recreated Personal Hell

The Strongman had the perfect road to remember, which would cut to the chase for Despair—Memory Lane with Deceit, her personal hell. "Let's see how she deals with it now," he thought. But just as he was rewinding the highlight reels from her bank of memories, Compassion extended His hand to Despair's eyes and slipped the pink glasses into place! And before he knew what had happened, Compassion pressed "play" on the selected memory. Hope, with her pink glasses firmly in place, saw that Deceit was really scared of a life that he couldn't control. Hope absently said, "I recognize this place. Yet somehow, this remembering looks and feels distinctly different, interesting even." She marveled as the memories kept unfolding before her eyes.

Hope saw that early on in his life, her father, Deceit, made a partnership with Fear. The thing with Fear, It's sneaky — those enraptured by fear don't realize that a partnership has been formed! Nor does one know that it's not really a "partnership" at all. She saw that Fear is a ruthless Taskmaster with its own pair of dark glasses. Fear's glasses had been worn by generations before Deceit. To be quite honest, everyone seemed to have a pair of Fear's dark glasses; they were all similarly boring. Each distinctly powerful to every generation that wore them. Fear's eyewear was so common that the wearers didn't know they had anything over their eyes! It was an ASTONISHING awareness that Hope was seeing while wearing Compassion's pink glasses!

Hope had never seen that reality before as she looked through her new lenses. Something started growing in her heart.

> The thing with fear, it's sneaky—those enraptured by fear don't realize that a partnership has been formed!

She wasn't quite sure what it was, but she liked how it felt even if she couldn't identify it. Compassion knew exactly what was happening and continued observing and taking notes.

The Strongman was growing impatient with Hope. Things weren't going as planned! While she watched, she wasn't crying or cursing her father, but there were glistening tears in her eyes! Keep the memory rolling, bitterness and woundedness will come eventually; he was sure of it!

Hope safely watched memories through her pink lenses, all the while, her heart was quivering with something other than fear.

Fear controlled Deceit with irrational outbursts, often accompanied by a shove that would send anyone nearby sprawling across the floor. More than once, Deceit had battered Martyr and her daughters into submission. Despair was now seeing the last violent incident that she endured. She knew this memory very well. She remembered being knocked to the ground and quickly getting back up, raising her chin in defiance. That didn't go well for her. Before she knew it, with a loud "smack" to her cheek, she was back on the floor!

Martyr was behind her crying out, "Stop getting up! Stay down! Just STAY DOWN!!" No, that would've been the easy route, and that's not how Despair did anything! To the astonishment of both Martyr and Deceit, Despair picked herself right back up, wiped her face, and practically taunted him to hit her again! Hope remembered this was the only time, Martyr tried to intervene on her behalf.

"Don't you EVER hit her again!" roared Martyr! Evidently, it really scared Deceit because he never hit Despair again after that day.

It was a PERFECT memory for The Strongman to remind Hope about as he tried to push her into an emotional upheaval! "Your father hurts you, hits you, kicks you down the hallway! He hates you!" The Strongman screamed.

But Hope, not Despair, was the one who saw the memory. Hope saw the entire exchange from an entirely different perspective through shimmering pink lenses that sat gently atop her strong nose. She could see Fear flinging Deceit around like a puppet on a string. Tears stung her eyes as she whisked away a stray curl that had fallen across her forehead. She felt sad for Deceit. She felt something bloom in her heart for them all. It felt warm and oddly comforting.

> Hope saw the exchange from a different perspective through shimmering pink lenses that sat gently atop her

The Strongman saw Hope's perspective of the memory FLIP right before his eyes! He was enraged!! Compassion had turned it upside right AGAIN!!

Quickly, before anything else could get messed up, he shifted the memory to one that occurred years later. Despair was leaving The Town of Silence. She had some crazy idea that her voice was good and that she was going to sing. She had an invitation to fly far, far away, and she intended to take it. Deceit wasn't at all pleased with this daughter of his. Despair seemed to have become Defiant over the years.

"If you leave, you'll be alone, and I will forget you," Deceit snapped. His face was blank, void of expression, but his words cut like a knife as they echoed in Despair's ears. She was leaving regardless of his threat. She didn't know how but she knew that this one was gonna hurt. She would leave. She would sing. She would live. She would succeed.

Although there were lingering thoughts swirling around in her mind, "What if I didn't succeed?" If she failed, if she suffered so terribly from the loneliness of having been forgotten, she could always return. Martyr always returned home after she ran away. There was always a possibility of "going home" tucked deeply into a corner of her heart. That is until she learned that Deceit and Martyr got rid of all of Despair's belongings. There was nothing to return "home" to anymore. She would never call The Town of Silence "home" again.

The stinging memory felt and looked starkly different through the glasses Compassion kept placing over her eyes. It's as if the glasses translated her vision into an entirely new awareness and flipped everything inside out and upside right!

Hope heard the words from her Dad through a different filter, almost as if they had been auto-tuned! She blinked hard while thinking, "Maybe there was an earpiece on the side of my glasses, and I just didn't notice it until now." These were the words she heard: "If you leave, I will miss you terribly, and I don't know how to handle my feelings. I will hurt so badly that I'll try to think of something or someone else, so I won't be reminded of how much I miss you! Please don't go. I love you."

Those weren't words from Deceit. Those were words from her Dad.

Standing there beside Compassion, she experienced this journey down Memory Lane from an awareness that surprised her. The blossom in her heart was taking root deeply as Hope whispered, "I love you too, Dad."

> Hope heard the words from her Dad through a different filter, almost as if they had been auto-tuned.

Again, it was as if the light had flickered and time folded over on itself. Now everything she saw was tinted with the most glorious shade of pale pink, like the pink that can only be found on the edge of a breath-taking sunset if you look at precisely the perfect moment. Compassion, ever-present, gently smiled and noted the moment in the little notebook with the quick flick of a pen.

Curiously, Hope noticed the pen for the first time. It was pink also —

pink marble as a matter of fact. "That's funny," she thought, "I'm certain that I've seen that pen somewhere before! In a dream, perhaps?" She couldn't quite place the memory, but she knew that it was significant. Not quite able to put her finger on it, Hope made a mental note to investigate the "pink pen" later. Soon she would remember, she dreamed of this pen on 9.19.19.

"Nevertheless, always-the-more!" She thought as she breathed a deeply hopeful breath. That was one of her mottos or declarations if you'd call it that. "Nevertheless, always-the-more." and off she went, reveling in the newfound memory of just how loved she'd been by her Dad, even though he didn't have the words to express it. Deceit was gone, and all she saw was Dad.

Nevertheless,
always-the-more!

Just outside of her view, Compassion jotted something else down with the weighty pink pen.

The Strongman disappointingly recognized that Hope had

completely reframed that trip down Memory Lane! She didn't cave into bitterness and woundedness like he thought she would. The awareness of her strength as "Hope" and NOT "Despair" actually caused The Strongman TO SHRINK!

The Strongman wailed as if in excruciating pain! He, in fact, HAD shrunken by at least 2 inches and was noticeably more shriveled than before! He wasn't very tall to begin with either. He appeared very scary if you had on the Fear glasses. That was it! It wasn't "her strength" at ALL; it was those pink glasses!!

"Maybe I went too far down Memory Lane," The Strongman thought, "She'd had too much time to think, and her memory has forgotten the sting of a good slap!"

> Compassion was right there, ever-present, and always observant.

Wracking his feeble brain to craft a new plan, he burst aloud, "I know! I'll bring it a little closer to home with a visitor from her past!" Let's call the visitor "Auntie," surely, she'll bring a shocking revelation of how the family had always thought her life would turn out! And maybe a tragedy will fall into my lap; I never waste a good tragedy, to manipulate my subjects back under my thumb! A visitor from her past will be perfect! Her sickeningly sweet little life will be no match for a visitor from Memory Lane. We'll truly see how she "sees" THEM!!"

He was practically giddy with his thoughts and was too consumed with a sickening thrill to notice that Compassion was right there, ever-present, and always observant.

She "SEES"

What The Strongman did know is that Hope SEES most things very differently now. She sees things forward and backward all the time! She was born with a particular anomaly that many perceive as a "disability"—she's "dyslexic." She didn't really know that there was a legitimate reason for her strangely backward way of seeing. She just figured out how to live with it. Not only did she figure out how to live with it, but she also learned how to thrive and succeed! In fact, she was quite skilled at finding "the instead" that was tucked into every seemingly backward situation.

You could say that dyslexia opened Hope's eyes to a gift of sorts. Hope LOVED palindromes. Let me explain, a palindrome is something that is the same forward and backward or is the same when it's right side up or upside down. Take the word "SEES," for example. It's a palindrome. You can read it forward and backward, and it still reads the same. Consider the word "MOM," if you flip it upside down, the mirror-image reads "WOW," it's a palindrome. Hope "SEES" them everywhere! In words, number patterns, and even natural structures, Hope sees palindromes as gifts for dyslexic people.

So, when The Strongman set out to mess with how she "SEES" the "visitors," he had no idea that he was setting himself up for disappointment.

Exploit & Twist or Twist & Exploit?

The Strongman has always had a "budget." A budget of time. A budget of resources. A budget of limitation and of limited power. The budget was imposed by I AM, who has NO budget of any kind. Zip! Zilch! Nada! And it completely undoes The Strongman! However, because of the "budget" constraints, The Strongman has always fancied himself to be a master manipulator who focused upon the same boring tools of "exploit & twist" and "use the generational fear glasses." "It works, so why try anything else?" he often encouraged himself with thoughts like this.

The Strongman has exploited everything that these puny humans have ever encountered. He has twisted perspectives and taken credit for all sorts of things, mostly because he just didn't want them to figure out that he had NO POWER except that he could persuade these simpletons to give their power to him. They gave up their power easily once their generational "fear glasses" were in place. The Strongman just had to press hard enough on something, or someone, until they questioned The Truth, that Creation itself daily declares for all to see. That's where those "dark fear glasses," laden with lenses of bitterness, offense, suspicion, and control, made his job much easier. He didn't have to work hard because those simpering fools did his job FOR him most of the time, and they couldn't even see what they'd fallen for in the end! And not only that, it didn't impact his budget at ALL because he didn't have to do the work! His boring little trick had worked for millennia on human and heavenly beings alike! He'd built himself a hoard of "dark glasses" wearers, and yet those DANG "pink glasses" worn by ONE stupid girl were BLOWING HIS BUDGET and ruining his day!

> ... The Strongman knows the truth too and even he has hope.

You see, The Strongman knows The Truth too, and even he has hope. He hopes that he can twist The Truth just enough for it to SOUND like truth and then use it to cheat The Beloveds out of the inheritance that belongs to them. A psalmist recorded these words in a book that was written before time was created, and interestingly the address for this Truth is a palindrome 19:1: "God's splendor is a tale that is told; His testament [story] is written in the stars. Space itself speaks His story every day through the marvels of the heavens. His truth is on tour in the starry vault of the sky, showing His skill in creation's craftsmanship." A palindrome narrated by The Master "Imaginator" Himself - written down by His friend David.[1]

Auntie and The Fever

Hope always looked up to Auntie. She was successful according to the gauge of success. She lived in a nice house, was married, had successful children. She was well regarded in the community. They hadn't seen each other in at least ten years or more, both of whom had long left The Town of Silence behind.

Hope was thrilled to host her in her home, the one she built with Prince Charming. Truly her life had become like a fairytale—the flower garden, the adoring husband, the happy children. Nothing at all like the home and family where she'd grown up. Hope secretly longed for approval from her, and surely Auntie would be proud of her success!

Ever watchful from the corner of her memory, Compassion took his position as the doorbell rang. The scene resembled a boxing match. Two opponents, each in opposite corners of the ring. The Strongman was taunting Compassion with hyped-up boastings of his previous victories.

"Round One, you simpering fool! You're going down! It's going to be a KNOCKOUT punch that will declare me the WINNER! I've never lost with this one! She will feel the gut-punch first and then a blow to her mind that will ring her bell!" Compassion simply smiled and said, "We'll see."

> As the two women exchanged pleasantries, The Strongman called out to Compassion, "Watch this!"

Hope was barefoot with a baby girl on her hip as she answered the door. It was surreal that Auntie was on her doorstep. A genuine smile ear to ear spread across both of their faces as they folded each other up in a hug that felt as natural as the sunshine! It was perfect!

As the two women exchanged pleasantries, The Strongman called out to Compassion, "Watch this."

Hope had prepared a tasty lunch to share with Auntie. She was so proud to let her see her life. Between sips of cool water that Hope had handed to her, the first gut-punch landed. "What a beautiful home and family, you have Despair. (Auntie still called her Despair, because she didn't yet know of her transformation.) You know we always thought you would be the one who wouldn't amount to anything. But look at you! You're beautiful! We never expected that!" said Auntie with a smile.

Hope blinked hard and thought for sure that she must've heard her wrong. Did she just say that she thought I'd never become anything? Surely not. "Thank you," Hope responded, with a slight smile, as she raised her glass to hide the fact that she just needed to swallow the conflicting feelings that were cascading through her brain. "YES! Gut punch!" squealed The Strongman. "It'll only take one more punch to knock her out!"

Compassion raised an unimpressed eyebrow. "We'll see," the same reply as before.

Auntie continued, "Oh, you're welcome! We thought you'd be that trailer park girl with a bunch of babies from different guys and no husband. But look at you! One husband, beautiful babies, and a real house in a neighborhood! So beautiful!"

> Compassion raised an unimpressed eyebrow, "We'll see."

Silently, Hope willed herself with some internal coaching to stay present in the moment. "Just keep smiling. Stuff all these feelings down. You can do this! Don't let anyone see." She coached herself as she smiled and kept eating the meal that she'd so excitedly prepared. "Thank you, Auntie. I'm so very happy. I could never have dreamed that I'd have such an amazing life." She replied to the backhanded compliment. Hope's head was spinning! In Auntie's world, she guessed that it was okay to insult someone if you completely bookend the insult with nice-sounding words!

"And there's the KNOCKOUT! Bring on the bitterness," as The Strongman began the countdown that signifies defeat. Compassion, still unimpressed, had the most tender look on his face as Prince Charming entered the room. The eyes of Compassion caught the gaze of The Strongman with a flash, and The Strongman stammered to a halt! The countdown to defeat stopped!

Prince Charming sat down beside Hope, and suddenly, the fog that had engulfed her mind cleared. His presence had that effect on her. He was a stabilizer that loved her back to life years before. He could lend the peace in his heart effortlessly. That was but one of the many things that Hope always loved about him.

Her pink lensed glasses almost glowed at that very moment. It was as if the mirrored lenses allowed Hope to SEE through the love of Prince Charming! She wasn't quite sure HOW that was happening, but she wasn't about to give up the posture from which she was experiencing this unexpected visitor. All the "backhanded compliments" simply bounced off the mirrored lenses. What Hope saw sitting across from her was simply "Auntie," and she really WAS proud of all that Hope had achieved in her life!

Compassion simply winked at The Strongman, but one would have thought that he'd been poked with a fiery arrow the way that he screamed and howled!

> Memory Lane was a pleasure that felt much like the redemption of every moment her pink lensed eyes beheld.

Becoming familiar with the "dance" patterns of "Memory Lane," Hope could rarely be found without her pink lensed glasses. It was as if she were running a race, effortlessly awash with every hue of color imaginable. Memory Lane was a pleasure that felt much like the redemption of every moment her pink lensed eyes beheld. "What an extraordinary gift it is to be one who truly SEES!" she exclaimed aloud as the memory glistened before her.

"NO!" wailed The Strongman, who appeared from out of thin air, "NO, you stupid little fool! It isn't a GIFT! It is a PUNISHMENT! It is a reminder of your horribly despairing life as a VICTIM of circumstances beyond your control!!"

But Hope couldn't hear or even detect the previously dominant voice that had manipulated her every move during the early frozen years of her life. She smiled with satisfied contentment, knowing full well that Goodness and Mercy both preceded and followed her every step now.[18] Her awareness was so profound she LOOKED for them every moment, past or present. To her utter delight, they were there! Hope could see that she had been redefined!

Compassion moved into the foreground of Memory Lane and stood in-between every vision that flashed before Hope's eyes. His maneuver infuriated The Strongman so terribly that he shriveled a bit and then simply vanished into thin air with a whooshing "POOF-FAH!" sound, and just like that, The Strongman was gone! Albeit temporarily, but still gone!

Remember what The Strongman said about "never wasting an opportunity to exploit a good tragedy"? The next opportunity to be exploited would be a fever, the 104-degree fever that lingered for days and days. The one that caused her daughter's brain to swell out of her skull. The fever that required Hope to hold her infant daughter as she screamed herself hoarse for three unsuccessful spinal taps! The fever that happened when Prince Charming almost couldn't be found to bail her out of this trauma!

"That'll do." He thought. "I'll try and kill her child." The Strongman had tried to kill important babies before, he was an expert at "steal, kill, and destroy."

Kill Her Baby

This memory would be a tricky one, and the attempt to pull this one off was hitting his budget hard! The Strongman remembered the entire event, but he planned to remind Hope of her disparaging life as a VICTIM of circumstances beyond her control. He hoped that the pink lenses that he couldn't knock off her face would somehow morph into those of RED-EYED ANGER! The Strongman could only hope. It was as if at that moment, he forgot that "hope, apart from God, isn't a tactic."

Hope's daughter had been sick with a lingering fever that just wouldn't let go. She did everything that she knew to do. She prayed. She called the doctor, who gave her all sorts of advice like: give her baby cool baths and a particular medicine every 4 hours before off-handedly adding, "these things usually pass." Hope didn't like the doctor very much at that moment. It felt as if he were diminishing her intuition and just blowing her off! "A 104-degree fever is NO JOKE," she seethed as she angrily hung up the phone!

The Strongman, totally engrossed in the memory of her outburst, completely overlooked the fact that the tint in her pink lenses didn't flicker or shake as Hope relived the crushing three days of helplessness.

After three days of sleepless wrestling with fear of the unknown,

Hope took her limp baby girl, along with her three-year-old brother, to the doctor's office in person. She would not be shrugged off by some stupid man who implied that she was overreacting!

"What did HE know about Mothering?! NOTHING!!" Hope was unstoppable in her intentionality to get some answers!
They quickly surmised that this was no ordinary fever, and this Little Miss had fluid on her brain that caused the soft spot on her tiny little skull to swell! Hope's daughter was unofficially diagnosed with Meningitis!

The only way to determine if it was bacterial or viral was to poke a hole in her spinal column, to remove the excess fluid for testing! Everything happened in slow motion and fast-forwarded simultaneously! It was shocking and altogether, horrible!

Even watching the memory, hand in hand with Compassion, silent tears slipped down Hope's cheeks from beneath the mirrored lenses.

Hope held her screaming baby perfectly still while the doctor, the one who had dismissed Hope's concerns for the past three days, made TWO unsuccessful attempts to puncture her spinal column! The screaming was unbearable for Hope! The only thoughts rushing through her mind were, "I can do this; it will save her life" and "please don't let my baby die!"

The staff called for a different doctor to help in the middle of the frenzy—the third attempt WAS successful! They drained the fluid that caused her brain to swell, then the baby was either limp from pain or relief that the intrusion into her spine had stopped. Her heart-wrenching cries ceased as Hope cradled Little Miss in her arms, with tears streaming down her face. The next step was to go IMMEDIATELY to The Children's Hospital, for quarantine and treatment as meningitis is very contagious and potentially deadly, depending on the strain.

> Her heart-wrenching cries ceased as Hope cradled Little Miss in her arms, with tears streaming down her face.

When Hope and her children arrived at the doctor's office, she and her daughter were whisked into a treatment room while her three-year-old son was looked after by the nursing staff. Hope had tried unsuccessfully to contact Prince Charming before the ordeal began. In the middle of the drama unfolding with Hope and her daughter, there was a desperate attempt by the staff to contact Prince Charming! He needed to know what was happening, and he needed to come to get their three-year-old son so Hope could go to the hospital! They were unsuccessful in locating him but left desperate messages for him to call the doctor's office ASAP!

> Hope kissed her son in that moment of complete audacity and did the only thing her head was screaming at her to do.

The nurse who had been making all the calls locked eyes with Hope and made an unforgettable offer! "Hope, I know you! We go to the same church! My little boy knows your little boy. Give me your son and the phone number of your emergency contact, and I'll make sure to get him safely taken care of!"

Hope kissed her son in that moment of complete audacity and did the only thing that her head was screaming at her to do! She had a limp baby in one arm, a bag of spinal fluid in her hand, and she gave her three-year-old with a phone number to a stranger!

Flinging the door to the office wide open, she bounded across the parking lot toward her car, only to hear screeching tires and grinding brakes!! It was Prince Charming!! He'd gotten the messages and immediately came rushing to the aid of two of the most important people in his life, his wife and daughter!

Hope was stoic until the moment he started to pray!

"God, we are asking you for healing! We trust you, and we know that Little Miss is just on-loan to us and whatever Your outcome is, we trust You! Amen." with a voice shaking with fear of the unknown, Prince Charming prayed.

"NO!! NO!! She's not on loan, and whatever is NOT WHAT I WANT!! HEAL HER!!" now "Despair's" voice wailed from Hope's mouth! The

Strongman loved this!! "Come on, anger!" he shouted at the recollection that was playing across the screen.

They had both seen undisputed miracles before! Hope had prayed for a dying baby in a third-world country, and it was miraculously HEALED! Now she wanted HER MIRACLE!! "God, you cannot take Little Miss back simply because she's "on loan" to us as her parents!" her words came out like spitting bullets.

They sped through crowded streets and arrived at the emergency center with a team waiting for them when they arrived. They required another spinal tap to confirm the diagnosis! It was INSANE, and Hope was even MORE ADAMANT about receiving her miracle!!

She didn't care who listened as she called on all her inheritance as a daughter of I AM and in the name of His Son! She didn't care that the doctor didn't believe in I AM or miracles! She prayed in a language that cuts through the atmosphere of time and space and went straight to the heart of I AM! She did what she knew to do as she held her limp baby for one more excruciating stab into her spine! It was more than Hope could bear, and the dam of tears and words burst forth!

"Thank you, God, that your signs, wonders, and miracles follow those that love You[2] and call on you through The Son!" her thankful gratitude punched a gaping hole in The Strongman's proverbial boat! She continued. "You are faithful, God, and we love You! I am filled with an overflowing, cascading HOPE." The gushing flow of Spirit inspired words was continuing to overtake The Strongman as she worshipped through tears over her limp Little Miss.

As the memories came in like a flood, The Strongman sensed that his proverbial boat was about to sink. So, he tried to distract Hope with the offenses of previously disappointing exchanges with "pastors" who had let her down in the hours that followed. The one that came to the hospital and didn't return with promised necessities that Hope had asked him to bring. That should do it!

> As the memories came in like a flood, The Strongman sensed that his proverbial boat was about to sink.

"'People of God' always let you down, you sniveling idiot! God disappoints you! Don't you forget that!" he spit out through gritted teeth. Hope remembered and smiled a little smile at what was about to come.

The waiting for test results in the dull, colorless room in the isolation unit seemed endless. They had decided to treat the baby for both viral and bacterial meningitis, the test results didn't matter, but they did need confirmation. Hope's daughter had been stripped down to nothing but a diaper. She was lying still almost lifeless on a pale green sheet covered bed. Her translucent skin has covered with sensors that were connected to wires and machines that made unnatural noises. They prepped her for the IV treatments as they waited for the medicine to come from the pharmacy. Yet, in the waiting, it was as if Hope was painting the dull walls with her words of worship and gratitude.

> Beloved is your truest identity!

Compassion simply stood. Pink pen in hand, writing words that appeared to glisten with a golden-pink hue, dancing as if alive, "She SEES."

"I am The Beloved of The Lord" [24] this is my truest identity! "You are

my God that never disappoints!"[3] "Because You ARE God, I believe in

her healing before I can see it."[4] Hope whispered with confidence that

shook everyone in the room, including those on the other side of the

glassed-in space. And just like that, her previously pale and limp

Little Miss sat up! Eyes wide and focused, cheeks pink and flushed!

The doctor, the one who had attempted the first and second spinal

taps in the pediatric office, rushed into the room and exclaimed,

"THIS is not the same baby that I saw just a few hours ago! The

treatment must've worked!" To which Hope replied, "Oh yes, it is,

AND they haven't begun any treatments!! It's a miracle!!" She

exclaimed with a steadfast joy!

Apparently, the doctor had never experienced anything like this

before, as he stammered and stuttered his way through a lame series

of possibilities that he suggested had happened. Still, Hope and

Prince Charming knew EXACTLY what occurred!

At that precise moment, a certain Strongman was experiencing a bit of personal trauma himself! It was apparent that seasickness might be overtaking the previously confident Strongman, he was a curious shade of puce! She couldn't really tell what was happening to him, but it sounded as if his feet might possibly come hurling out of his mouth the way he was wrenching! Compassion silently chuckled at the sight he witnessed.

Everything shifted at that moment. The Strongman, in his sinking boat, couldn't bear the weight of the "memory of the fever" any longer, and it was as if he'd been sucked out of the wide-open gash that Hope's last statement had torn in his feeble vessel. He was simply whisked from the inside out into Hope's sea of gratitude because she, in fact, SEES.

Two worlds collided,
flipping the foundation in her
heart and mind.

What had long been her

primary sense of "awareness,"

the natural atmosphere, gave

way to the spiritual

atmosphere's greater reality!

Part Three

Upside Right!

In that moment, Hope had no idea that her foundations

had been restored to their Divine intentions. She had no idea that

two worlds had collided, one spiritual and one natural. There hadn't

just been a collision, but the foundation flipped position[5] in her heart

and mind. What had long been her primary sense of "awareness," the

natural atmosphere, gave way to the spiritual atmosphere's greater

reality! Now she saw everything UPSIDE RIGHT with the eyes of her

spirit! Awareness changed everything!

Prince Charming collected their son from the Godmother's house,

who had also prayed for "his baby" (as he lovingly called her) to be

healed. The stranger who helped Hope in her moments of crisis

became a Sweet Friend that day. Hope and her daughter, Little Miss,

stayed quarantined for the required time during treatment for

contagious meningitis even though a full recovery came BEFORE the medications began. They were known all over the hospital as "The Miracle Meningitis Baby and her Momma."

To this day, Little Miss has no memory of the trauma that she endured, nor is there anything lingering from that encounter.

Memory Lane was a complete BUST! The Strongman's budget for Hope's destruction was SHOT!

> It took The Strongman YEARS to recover from his skirmish with Hope. He avoided her like she had The Plague!

Not only that, it took The Strongman YEARS to recover from his skirmish with Hope. He avoided her like she had The Plague! Dealing with her was far too expensive and costly to his fear budget! It simply wasn't worth it for him to mess with her.

"No matter," he thought, "time will bring me something eventually. I've still got a few cards to play with Hope!" He continued to stubbornly refuse to accept that she really received a new name.

The City of Trees and Cankerworms

There are two majestic and noble magnolia trees that stand more than 70 feet tall at the home of The Beloveds. These trees are believed to be around 50 years old, almost as old as Hope and Prince Charming. The leathery leaves are a deep dark green with a shiny, almost waxy appearance on the top and a rich earthy brown beneath. For a moment, in the late Spring, these stoic sentries will bloom with the most glorious and gigantic flowers that have anywhere from 6 to 15 petals apiece. It's curious to note that these humungous trees bear their flowers individually and not in clusters like most other flowering trees. Not only that, the bloom rarely lasts more than 24 hours if it's cut from the tree. Hope learned that it's best to enjoy her graceful companions' noble beauty by leaving the blossoms on the trees.

Living in The City of Trees had both benefits and bothers. The trees provided shelter and shade to all manner of winged creatures and four-legged critters. The birds of every color found safety to build their nests and deposit their eggs, those that would be the next generation of songbirds to sing their beautiful songs of freedom and joy. Squirrels with their fluffy tails and silly antics benefited from the canopies high above the dangers lurking down below and up above. The benefits that the trees provided were, and still are, plentiful. The bothers remain unnoticed until they show up as unwelcome interlopers called Cankerworms!

Cankerworms can strip a tree of its glorious leaves almost before you know they are there! The bare tree is then exposed to sickness and disease. The cankerworm alone can bring death to the tree.

The Strongman hadn't visited The Beloved's for a while, he patiently waited for a cankerworm to exploit. In his absence, Hope had grown strong, extremely strong as a matter of fact, and was nearly unrecognizable to the diminishing Strongman. He had been shrinking for years, and it was noticeable when he showed up in her life again.

"No matter," he thought, "I have a little worm for your towering trees.

We'll see how tall you stand after the swarm has devoured you and your trees are stripped bare. My worm is called cancer, and it will eat those who Hope loves from the inside out."

In his glee, The Strongman failed to see that awareness had flipped the posture in Hope's heart of how she saw her formerly frozen years in The Town of Silence.

These days Hope always had her shiny pink lensed glasses on, and Compassion was her constant companion and coach in The City of Trees. With this new awareness, Martyr, the one who had named her daughter after her enemy, was now simply Mom, and she was desperate for a blessing while dying from cancer herself.

Hope remembered and felt the sting of every careless word spit at her over the years. All the while, her memories were being filtered through Compassion as if she had an earpiece in her ear, which infuriated The Strongman to no end!

Then the phone rang. It was Prince Charming. He had some bad news. He had cancer too.

Signal showtime for The Strongman! Manipulate. Exploit. Twist. Steal. Kill. Destroy.

Hope's immediate response was, "This is not our inheritance! It is not our portion! MORE abundant life is our portion! We refuse to host cancer even one day!" The Beloved's held each other and cried tears of many names. Bitterness. Anger. Confusion. Questioning.

> They cried until their tears gave way to confidence, peace, trust, and compassion.

They cried until their tears gave way to confidence, peace, trust, and compassion.

They put their confidence in the goodness of God. They were filled with peace, knowing that they were firmly held with an unshakable hope. Trust in The One who knows the number of hairs on their heads. Compassion, He knows what they are walking through, and He always provides even if it's in mysterious ways.

The cankerworm that visited Prince Charming, the one called cancer, was evicted, and made homeless. The recovery was long and difficult, but Hope and her Prince weathered the storm and emerged stronger together! The worm had left its mark on The Beloveds. However, it was completely eradicated and replaced by a soul-tattoo of the ever-present GOODNESS and nearness of God. Who had transformed "the mark of the worm" into a "billboard of EXTREME HOPE" for all to see!

The cankerworm that visited Martyr would claim her life. But not before the restoration that The Strongman didn't see coming!

Extreme Hope had completely transformed before her final visit to see Martyr! She was once Despair from The Town of Silence. Long ago Despair collided with The Creator of Everything meeting His Son in the middle of her mess and He remade everything in her life. She was refashioned in every way. She was transformed when she believed her true identity, which was hidden in The Son, waiting for her discovery. Extreme Hope was born as she fought her way out of her cocoon into freedom, with a heart of Compassion.

In a hospital room, surrounded by her sisters, Extreme Hope with the heart of Compassion released a blessing over Martyr's cancer-riddled body that transformed everyone listening! At that moment, the atmosphere shifted. Extreme Hope began to bless the one that had cursed her. The blessing was extravagant and lavish, authentic, and genuine, even thrilling Hope as she heard words being uttered with her own voice! Years of frozenness melted away, being replaced with a flame of love that burned bright and hot between Extreme Hope and her Mother, Martyr.

Mother was close to the gates of heaven and had lost her ability to reply, but she spoke with her tears. Hope could hear each tear as it trickled across her cheek. It was as if heaven kissed the earth, and all things were reconciled between them.

Everything and everyone, with breath, bore witness to what occurred supernaturally. Years of wrongs were forgiven as tears washed them away. The stains of offense simply faded away into memories with no sting.

Her reality had shifted again. Compassion wasn't standing alongside her, taking notes with the pink marble pen, as had been a familiar scene. The vine of Compassion had become firmly implanted in Hope's heart, and spectacularly, had become a mighty branch[14] that had been pruned so well that its FRUIT was abundant!

Hope learned something without even really knowing it. She came to know Jesus as "loving" and so her expectation was that she could both give and receive Love. She also came to know Him as good, relentlessly good. She constantly experienced His goodness even in the direst of situations. When Hope received Jesus as "Compassion," it was then that He knew that she knew Him as Emmanuel—God with us! [23]

> The awareness was staggering and simultaneously thrilling.

Hope realized that she and Mother were not the only ones who were transformed, her sisters were too! All this time, Success and

Oblivious had been having encounters with Compassion, and they continue to this very day. The awareness was staggering and simultaneously thrilling!

Not Really a Strongman After All

She could see that The Strongman was nothing more than a boring little imp, with tiny little arms that reminded her of the useless arms on the now extinct T-Rex. He was a creature like a round ball, no more than 2 feet tall, set on feeble sticks that slightly resembled legs. He was a faint reflection of who he was originally created to be. The

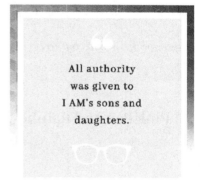

All authority was given to I AM's sons and daughters.

Strongman used to be the lead worshipper in heaven until he wanted to dethrone, I AM to take his place! He was banished from I AM's presence, all authority was stripped from him and given to I AM's sons and daughters instead. THAT's why he tries to be "The Strongman" and to trick them out of their inheritances!!

Hope felt compassion for the silly little Imp! Her "awareness" was the last straw for the former "Strongman." Her compassion consumed him since Love takes no account of a suffered wrong. Love simply loves because I AM loved us first. He made way for us to create heaven on Earth and host The Kingdom of God most spectacularly, through a relationship with His Son.[19] *"For this is how much God loved the world—he gave his one and only, unique Son as a gift. So now everyone who believes in him l will never perish but experience everlasting life. God did not send his Son into the world to judge and condemn the world, but to be its Savior and rescue all of humanity!"*

A Pink Pen and Rainbow Cakes — the 9.19.19 Dream

Extreme Hope finally remembered where she had seen Compassion's pink marble pen! During a dream, she was in an auditorium that was filled with people as far as her eye could see. The room was electrified with celebration and expectancy. The man on the stage was a well-known figure and a friend of I AM. He called out a man's name, and the crowd cheered as he excitedly wove his way to the front of the room where he was given a heavy pen, and a small white cake! Hope was part of this great gathering of witnesses to a lavish celebration of what appeared to be a culmination of years of faithfulness. Name after name was called, and the same sequence of events would be repeated. Her heart was overflowing with joy at watching the rewards and accolades handed out. The celebration was almost more than she could comprehend. Then Hope heard HER name called out! Those who were standing nearby all turned toward her, the applause was deafening. So much so that he called her name again, "Extreme Hope." His eyes fixed on her's, he motioned her to the front too!!

To her surprise, as she neared the platform, she was invited to join him front and center on the stage. That's not how everyone else received their gifts, but she was so caught up in the momentum of the moment that she practically skipped up the nine treads on the stairs leading to the stage.

With rosy cheeks and an ear-to-ear smile, Hope was centerstage and it felt like the whole world was watching as the man handed her a

Pink Marble fountain pen. Like the ones that leave an ink stain on the side of your finger! (It was EXACTLY the same pen that Compassion had been writing with throughout her entire journey, but she wouldn't realize it until a year later.)

Then the man turned around and retrieved a trolley that held a large white cake, identical to all others except for its size. It was TWICE the size. He handed her a silver cake knife and invited her to cut the cake right there as everyone watched. Hope cut into the cake with the weighty pink marble pen in her right hand and a large silver knife in her left, and light burst forth! Every hue of imaginable color spilled out, and the crowd went wild with celebration. It was as if they were endued with new vigor, and the sound reverberated through Hope's feet like she was standing on electricity! One more slice with the silver knife and a sliver of sweetness she had never tasted before lay on the plate before her! The white cake contained a raucous mix of every created color. The treasure prepared in advance for Hope was waiting for her to reveal it to the world! "Taste and see."[22]

Hope took a bite, and to her surprise, she understood this cake of many colors. Each color represented a season of her life, all mixed with honey and delicately seasoned with salt to bring out the sweetness the color contained.

Hope saw Memory Lane and The Town of Silence and could savor the sweetness that they contained. The Strongman had given up and surrendered to Compassion, as evidenced by the ribbon of pink woven through the marbled circus of color. Hope saw her family, every single member, in the soft hues on the edges of the intense colors contained in her cake. Hope saw the Land of Ideal and The City of Trees and remembered when she first met, I Am and His Son in a field of greener than green grass. A moment that was the most delicious delicacy Hope ever encountered.

Her dream was a foreshadowing of what lay ahead for Extreme Hope. She would know the complete restoration and redemption of every bitter tear that had ever fallen from her eyes—through this simple dream.

Extreme Hope has become the absolute expectation of God's

goodness showing up and showing off in, through, and for her.

Through the eyes of Compassion Extreme Hope was able to reconcile her world with pink lenses and a pink marble pen. Life truly IS prettier in pink!

Awareness really did change everything because SHE changed, from the inside out! Despair was transformed into Extreme Hope. Her life is a celebration—a triumph of love, beauty, and victory.

She is shiny & healed.

"

Extreme Hope is a reality that is seen by those who are radically convinced in the goodness of God as being their absolute expectation.

Part Four

Your Perfect Destiny!

Dear Friend

I wrote this story as an allegory, where the characters are "attributes," "feelings," or "character traits" rather than specific people. I chose this method so that you, the reader, could be "embedded into the story" since we are all the same kind of different. We have different names, different skin tones, different age groups, and yet altogether, we are the same kind of human, with frailties and feelings, yet full of unlimited possibilities.

Perhaps it worked, and you saw yourself as you read this story. Maybe you have experienced the deep betrayal of abandonment from someone who was supposed to love you unconditionally. My desire for you is to know that there is HOPE, the absolute expectation of the goodness of God, showing up and showing off for you! It's an extreme posture of heart, it's Extreme Hope!

Extreme Hope believes that God has something so marvelous in store for you that until any outcome hasn't been transformed into something so good and breathtakingly beautiful, it simply isn't the end yet. I call it "Instead." There is an "instead" tucked into every situation for the sons and daughters of God. The "instead" is part of your birthright, it's your inheritance.

Jesus is my reason for Extreme Hope, and He can be your's too! Do you remember in the very beginning of the story, all the way back when Despair was in the back of a dark moving van? There was a "Heavenly Agent" tucked into the shadows where Despair couldn't see. Jesus was the "Agent," but you probably already figured that out!

Jesus shows up in this story as a "Heavenly Agent," "The Son," "The Savior," "Wisdom," "Compassion," "Love," "Forgiveness," "The Way." God is "I AM" and "The Father," but you probably already knew THAT too! Wink!

Despair met Them once when she was a child. She went to church because she had no choice. She was a kid and had to do what she was told. Honestly, in those days, it was quite an escape for her to go to a church far away from her life's reality. She met Jesus there, and even though her life wasn't perfect, and she made more mistakes than she could count, Jesus never left, and He never disowned her. He remained faithful[20] because it's impossible for Him to disown Himself! I know it sounds unbelievable, but this is EXTREME Hope!

> And the good news is that there is never a pit so deep that God has not already been there and made a way for our rescue!

And the good news today is that there is never a pit so deep that God has not already been there and made way for our rescue! Jesus is that rescue! He meets us in our pit, in our mess, in our whatever, and He makes a way of escape where there seems to be no way! It's called Forgiveness through a relationship with Jesus.[16]

The Enemy of humanity is "The Strongman," but he's really not as "strong" as he thinks he is. He is boring, uncreative, and likes to bring division, confusion, and strife between the Heirs of the Kingdom of God. He loves control and manipulation. The Enemy has no power and he cannot take your life, he knows this, so he tries to get humanity to partner with him to bring death and destruction. One of the ways that he does this is through the lie of suicide. I know his lies all too well. The lies say that "your life isn't worth living" or "the lives of those I love will be better if I'm not alive." These whispers are LIES straight from Hell! If you are struggling with the lies of suicide and need help, please reach out.

The National Suicide Prevention Lifeline provides free and confidential emotional support to people in suicidal crisis or emotional distress 24 hours a day, 7 days a week, across the United States. Call the Lifeline at 1-800-273-8255.

A Marvelous Opportunity and Invitation

Religion is complicated. A Relationship with Jesus is simple.

Tell Him the truth about your life. I promise that He won't turn away in shame or disgust. He will look at you as Compassion Himself, with

Forgiveness and restoration because He took your mess and your despair to the cross with Him, then He died with it. He rose to LIFE, leaving the mess behind so that you could live FREE from The Strongman's prison!

Religion will say: "It can't be that easy!" Being in a relationship with Jesus is, in fact, that simple! The Awareness of this simplicity changes everything! I often say it like this:

"Jesus isn't afraid of your mess. He wants to walk with you and show you Who and How He is. As you walk along with Him, transformation is inevitable. As we become more aware of His great Love for us, that Awareness Changes Everything!"

Here's a simple way to invite Jesus into a relationship:

> *"Jesus, here's my mess and all of my mistakes. I'm sorry for the ways that I've tried to go through this life on my own. I believe that You are God's solution for me and a relationship with you is The Way to transform my mess into a masterpiece.*

I want to be your friend. I thank You for forgiving me, for

loving me, and for restoring me. Amen."

It really is that simple.

So, we find ourselves at the end of the story. Or do we? It is actually

an invitation to the beginning of YOUR story that Jesus wants to write

with you, as you look through the

eyes of Compassion.

> Since Compassion is
> who Jesus is, it is also
> who we are
> as his friends!

Now the journey into Awareness

begins! Remember, Awareness

Changes Everything.

As I wrote this allegory, I kept thinking about "swapping out my

glasses." I have glasses that I wear when I write. I have glasses that I

wear when I'm outside in the sun. I kept thinking about "putting on

compassion like a putting on a pair of glasses." Since Compassion is

who Jesus is, I would like to propose that we could "put on the eyes of

Compassion" and see through His perspective. Literally.

In my story Despair was transformed as she became accustomed to seeing through her "pink-tinted lenses of Compassion" when previously and unknowingly she'd been wearing the "dark lenses of Fear" that generations before her also wore.

Can you imagine what your life could look like with the "eyes of compassion"?! What could every relationship you have look like if your perspective was tinted with compassion? What about the way we interact with family members, neighbors, and coworkers? Is it possible that we could SEE that we're all the SAME beautiful shade of "pink/compassion," with unique hues and tones that decorate our skin? The possibilities for upgraded perspectives are endless when we look through the eyes of Compassion.

Let's dream bigger together for a moment. What could our cities, our states, our nations, and our governments look like if we intentionally partner with Compassion? It could look like a RECONCILIATION on a national, even a global scale!

Many people have heard "The Lord's Prayer" from Matthew 6 and perhaps even have it memorized. This is an excerpt of Matthew 6 from The Passion Translation (TPT) spoken by Compassion, Jesus: [9] Pray like this:

> "*Our Father, dwelling in the heavenly realms, may the glory of Your name be the center on which our lives turn. Manifest Your kingdom realm, and cause Your every purpose to be fulfilled on earth, just as it is fulfilled in heaven. We acknowledge You as our Provider of all we need each day Forgive us the wrongs we have done as we ourselves release forgiveness to those who have wronged us. Rescue us every time we face tribulation and set us free from evil. For You are the King who rules with power and glory forever. Amen.*"

I often wonder what "Manifesting Your kingdom realm and causing Your every purpose to be fulfilled on earth" could look like?

I would like to propose that it could look very much like a pair of pink-tinted glasses given to us by Compassion Himself that allow us to SEE through his eyes! Not only that, since Compassion is who He is, it is also who we are as His! Friends this is bigger than we can possibly imagine!

Perhaps you grew up poor. So did I. Perhaps you have been homeless. I have too. Perhaps you've been wrongfully or rightfully accused. So have I. Perhaps you've known success or failure and perhaps you're not perfect. I'm just like you. Compassion Himself knows all our details and has made a way for us to be reconciled.

It starts with me and you. Through the eyes of compassion, we can see that we're all the same kind of different.

After all, awareness changes everything.

What's next?

If you invited Jesus to make you into a masterpiece, tell someone and let them celebrate with you! Then, would you let me know? I'd love to celebrate with you too. Connect with me on my website www.LoriClifton.com, at "Lori Clifton | Imaginator" on Facebook, or Instagram @loriiclifton. More details about how to connect with me are on the "About the Author" page in this book.

Notes

The Passages & Palindromes that Speak of Our Eternal Inheritance

From The Passion Translation; The Amplified Bible - Classic Version;

and, The New International Version

1.   Psalm 19:1 TPT

"God's splendor is a tale that is told; His testament [story] is written

in the stars. Space itself speaks His story every day through the

marvels of the heavens. His truth is on tour in the starry vault of the

sky, showing His skill in creation's craftsmanship."

2. Acts 2:22 TPT

"Peter continued, "People of Israel, listen to the facts. Jesus, the

Victorious, was a Man on a divine mission whose authority was

clearly proven. For you know how God performed many powerful

miracles, signs, and wonders through him."

3. Romans 5:5 TPT

"And this hope is not a disappointing fantasy, because we can now experience the endless love of God cascading into our hearts through The Holy Spirit who lives in us!"

4. Hebrews 11:1 TPT

"Now faith brings our hopes into reality and becomes the foundation needed to acquire the things we long for. It is all the evidence required to prove what is still unseen."

5. 2 Thessalonians 3:3 TPT

"But the Lord is always faithful to place you on a firm foundation and guard you from The Evil One."

6. Colossians 2:2 NIV

My goal is that they may be encouraged in heart and united in love, so that they may have the full riches of complete understanding, in order that they may know the mystery of God, namely, Christ, [in whom are hidden all the treasures of wisdom and knowledge. I tell you this so that no one may deceive you by fine-sounding arguments.]

7. Colossians 1:15-17 TPT

He is the divine portrait, the true likeness of the invisible God, and the first-born heir of all creation. For through the Son everything was created, both in the heavenly realm and on the earth, all that is seen and all that is unseen. Every seat of power, realm of government, principality, and authority—it was all created through him and for his purpose! He existed before anything was made, and now everything finds completion in him.

8. Colossians 1:21-23 NIV

Even though you were once distant from him, living in the shadows of your evil thoughts and actions, he reconnected you back to himself. He released his supernatural peace to you through the sacrifice of his own body as the sin-payment on your behalf so that you would dwell in his presence. And now there is nothing between you and Father God, for he sees you as holy, flawless, and restored, if indeed you continue to advance in faith, assured of a firm foundation to grow

upon. Never be shaken from the hope of the gospel you have believed

in. And this is the glorious news.

The Supremacy of Christ

9. Colossians 1:15-20 TPT

He is the divine portrait, the true likeness of the invisible God, and

the first-born heir of all creation. For through the Son everything

was created, both in the heavenly realm and on the earth, all that is

seen and all that is unseen. Every seat of power, realm of government,

principality, and authority—it was all created through him and for

his purpose! He existed before anything was made, and now

everything finds completion in him.

He is the Head of his body, which is the church. And since he is the

beginning and the firstborn heir in resurrection, he is the most

exalted One, holding first place in everything. For God is satisfied to

have all his fullness dwelling in Christ. And by the blood of his cross,

everything in heaven and earth is brought back to himself—back to

its original intent, restored to innocence again!

10. Hebrews 1:3 TPT

The Son is the dazzling radiance of God's splendor, the exact expression of God's true nature—his mirror image! He holds the universe together and expands it by the mighty power of his spoken word. He accomplished for us the complete cleansing of sins, and then took his seat on the highest throne at the right hand of the majestic One.

10. Matthew 4:16, TPT

You who spend your days shrouded in darkness can now say, "We have seen a brilliant Light." And those who live in the dark shadow land of death can now say, "The Dawning Light arises on us."

The Tree of Life

11. Psalm 1:1-3, TPT

"What delight comes to the one who follows God's ways! He won't walk in step with the wicked, nor share the sinner's way, nor be found sitting in the scorner's seat. His pleasure and passion is remaining true to the Word of "I Am," meditating day and night in the true revelation of light. He will be standing firm like a flourishing tree planted by God's design, deeply rooted by the brooks of bliss, bearing fruit in every season of his life. He is never dry, never fainting, ever blessed, ever prosperous.

12. Proverbs 13:12, TPT

When hope's dream seems to drag on and on, the delay can be depressing. But when at last your dream comes true, life's sweetness will satisfy your soul.

13. Proverbs 13:13, TPT

Despise the word, will you? Then you'll pay the price and it won't be pretty! But the one who honors the Father's holy instructions will be rewarded.

14. John 15:5, TPT

"I am the sprouting vine and you're my branches. As you live in union with me as your source, fruitfulness will stream from within you.

15. John 15:15, NIV

"I no longer call you servants, because a servant does not know his master's business. Instead, I have called you friends, for everything that I learned from my Father I have made known to you. "

The Roman Road

16. Romans 3:23; 5:8, and 10:13, NIV (emphasis added)

"For all have sinned (messed up & made mistakes) and fall short of the glory of God."

"But God demonstrates his own love for us in this: While we were still sinners (still in our mess), Christ died for us."

"For, 'Everyone who calls on the name of the Lord will be saved.'"

17. Romans 4:18, NIV

Against all hope, Abraham in hope believed and so became the father of many nations, just as it had been said to him, "So shall your offspring be."

18. Psalm 23:6, AMP

"Surely goodness and mercy and unfailing love shall follow me all the days of my life, And I shall dwell forever [throughout all my days] in the house and in the presence of the Lord."

19. John 3:16 & 17, TPT

For this is how much God loved the world—he gave his one and only, unique Son as a gift. So now everyone who believes in him[l] will never perish but experience everlasting life. "God did not send his Son into the world to judge and condemn the world, but to be its Savior and rescue it!

20. 2 Timothy 2:13, NIV & TPT

"if we are faithless, he remains faithful, for he cannot disown himself." But even if we are faithless, he will still be full of faith, for he never wavers in his faithfulness to us!

21. Psalm 103 TPT

With my whole heart, with my whole life, and with my innermost being, I bow in wonder and love before you, the holy God! Yahweh, you are my soul's celebration. How could I ever forget the miracles of kindness you've done for me? You kissed my heart with forgiveness, in spite of all I've done. You've healed me inside and out from every disease. You've rescued me from hell and saved my life. You've crowned me with love and mercy. You satisfy my every desire with good things. You've supercharged my life so that I soar again like a flying eagle in the sky! You're a God who makes things right, giving justice to the defenseless. You unveiled to Moses your plans and showed Israel's sons what you could do. Lord, you're so kind and tenderhearted to those who don't deserve it and so patient with people who fail you! Your love is like a flooding river overflowing its banks with kindness. You don't look at us only to find our faults, just so that you can hold a grudge against us. You may discipline us for our many sins, but never as much as we really deserve. Nor do you get even with us for what we've done. Higher than the highest heavens— that's how high your tender mercy extends! Greater than the grandeur of heaven above is the greatness of your loyal love, towering over all who fear you and bow down before you! Farther than from a sunrise to a sunset—that's how far you've removed our guilt from us. The same way a loving father feels toward his children—that's but a sample of your tender feelings toward us, your beloved children, who live in awe of you. You know all about us, inside and out. You are mindful that we're made from dust. Our days are so few, and our momentary beauty so swiftly fades away! Then all of a sudden we're gone, like grass clippings blown away in a gust of wind, taken away to our appointment with death, leaving nothing to show that we were here. But Lord, your endless love stretches from one eternity to the other, unbroken and unrelenting toward those who fear you and those who bow facedown in awe before you. Your faithfulness to keep every gracious promise you've made passes from parents, to children, to grandchildren, and beyond. You are faithful to all those who follow your ways and keep your word. God's heavenly throne is eternal, secure, and strong, and his sovereignty rules the entire universe. So bless the Lord, all his messengers of power, for you are his mighty heroes who listen intently to the voice of his word to do it. Bless and praise the Lord, you mighty warriors, ministers who serve him well and fulfill his desires. I will bless and praise the Lord with my whole heart! Let all his works throughout the earth, wherever his dominion stretches, let everything bless the Lord!

22. Psalm 34:8 NIV

Taste and see that the Lord is good; blessed is the one who takes
refuge in him.

23. Matthew 1:21-23 TPT

She will give birth to a son and you are to name him 'Savior,' for he is
destined to give his life to save his people from their sins."
This happened so that what the Lord spoke through his prophet
would come true: Listen! A virgin[s] will be pregnant, she will give
birth to a Son, and he will be known as "Emmanuel, which means in
Hebrew, "God became one of us."

24. Deuteronomy 33:12, NIV

About Benjamin he said: "Let the beloved of the LORD rest secure in
him, for he shields him all day long, and the one the LORD loves
rests between his shoulders."

.

Cast of Characters

Deceit – The Earthly Father
Betrayal's – The Father's Family
Entitlement – Deceit's Brother
Confidence – Entitlement transformed after meeting The Young
Teacher

Martyr – The Mother
Suffering's – The Mother's family
Sympathy – Martyr's brother
Scorn – Martyr's brother
Bliss – Scorn's wife

Despair – Daughter of Martyr & Deceit
Success – Older Sister of Despair
Oblivious – Younger Sister of Despair
The Strongman – The Evil Ruler
Pride – The "Jailer," The Strongman in disguise
Distortion – Pride's "sister"
Defiance – Pride's "sister"
Relief – Suicide in disguise

I AM – God
The Throne – Where God sits, above the circle of the earth
Heavenly Agent – Love, Wisdom, The Young Teacher, Compassion,
Defender, The Son, The Savior, Jesus
Heirs to the Throne – Everyone who comes to God through Jesus
Hope – Despair transformed after meeting I AM and The Savior
Prince Charming – Beloved, Hope's Husband
Little Miss – Hope's Daughter

About the Author

It's a funny thing writing about myself. Just being transparent in this day and age can be scary because it seems that everyone has an opinion about one another that they feel compelled to share. Nevertheless, here goes!

I snapped a picture in front of the window in my office, it is raw & unedited, accurate, and authentically me. I see wrinkles like train tracks across my forehead from 52 years of many expressions. I see crepe-paper lines dancing at the corners of my eyes from 52 years of more smiles than tears. I see freckles from exposure to the southern sunlight that has left its fingerprint on my skin. I see a light in my eyes that is more than a reflection through the panes of glass. I see a smile that is content and confident declaring "I am loved."

I like the woman I see.

I've been told, "Because you're beautiful, people won't believe that you've ever had a hard life."

Believe me when I tell you that the description above was not always my reality. I have known pain, loss, betrayal, and disappointment. My life has had its share of calamity and disasters that I didn't choose and could not change.

However, 34 years ago I collided with God, The Author of Hope Himself became my Divine Mentor and ever since He's been teaching me about my inheritance, as His daughter, and how to live "disaster proof from the inside out." I confidently declare, "I will not hesitate to live bravely."

Always learning. Always growing. Always advancing.

Awareness changes everything!

It is my heart to proclaim this message of Awareness that changes everything and Extreme Hope with any with everyone that has breath in their lungs! It would be my honor to walk with you through The Awareness Suite.

Dive deeper into AWARENESS with Lori Clifton at

www.loriclifton.com through:

The Awareness Suite

Hearing God for Yourself

Establishing your Culture with

7 foundational conversations all about your inheritance

~ it's your BIRTHRIGHT to Hearing God for Yourself.

The ABC's of Hope

Exercising your Communication skills and

co-authoring with God

Disaster proofing your life from the inside out through

The ABC's of Hope.

WifI Training - "What if Instead..."

Connection is never a problem when you become a WifI Expert

after gaining this "What if Instead..." Life Strategy.

Conversations with The Author of Hope

Putting it all together while drafting off a

Culture of Connection & Communication

~ life strategies ~

from the perspective of The Author of Hope.

Thank You's and Acknowledgements

To my dearest husband Scott, 26 years ago on the 26th day of the month, you married me on my 26th birthday, and changed my life forever! I don't have the words to express how deeply thankful I am for the extravagant gift that you have been to me for these past years! Your constant support of who I am and your belief in my purpose has been a magnificent example of sacrificial and unconditional love.

During these past 26 years, our love story created three stellar children who have grown into beautiful young adults. Our eldest son Alex has learned how to love, value, and celebrate others by walking in your footsteps to become a husband to Taylor. Our daughter, Mali, has grown into a brave and determined young woman who knows how to pursue the dreams in her heart with a tenacious ferocity that makes me smile. Nicholas, our youngest son, from the very beginning has been a bundle of generosity and exceeding joy. Each one of our children are marked by a fierce loyalty to their family and loved-ones, as well as to God Himself.

Thank you, Scott, Alex & Taylor, Mali, and Nicholas, for simply being "you!" I love you all dearly! We truly are The Beloved of The Lord.

To my sisters, Michelle and Kim, for living and loving well!

To my Mom and Dad, who are celebrating me from heaven, I love you deeply!

To Emily, Briana, and Esther, my "bonus Southern sisters," who have been constant "cowbells of encouragement" over the many years of our friendships! Everyone NEEDS MORE "cowbells!"

To Hannah, Lana, Maree, Nic, and Sabrina for being fellow dreamers and God-lovers that pull the unseen into reality. Our friendships have crossed time zones and oceans connecting our hearts in the most extraordinary fashion—Canada, South Africa, Australia, New Zealand, and Great Britain. North Carolina will be with you one day!

To Ann and the Kingdom Mastermind Lovelies, we are WORTHY!

To Charlana for believing in this project, for making space for me to stand alongside you, and for calling me "Honey" in a way that makes me feel like I am so thoroughly known and loved! This book is the first of many "adventures" that we are meant to share together!

Finally, to Compassion— Emmanuel, God with us — the Lover of my soul, Jesus, thank you for pursuing me with reckless abandon! Thank you for bridging time and space to rescue and restore me so that I became the Extreme Hope that I was created to be!

Made in the USA
Las Vegas, NV
14 March 2021

19540071R00079